SECRETS TO HAPPINESS

WORKBOOK

Table of Contents

Layer 1
Desire

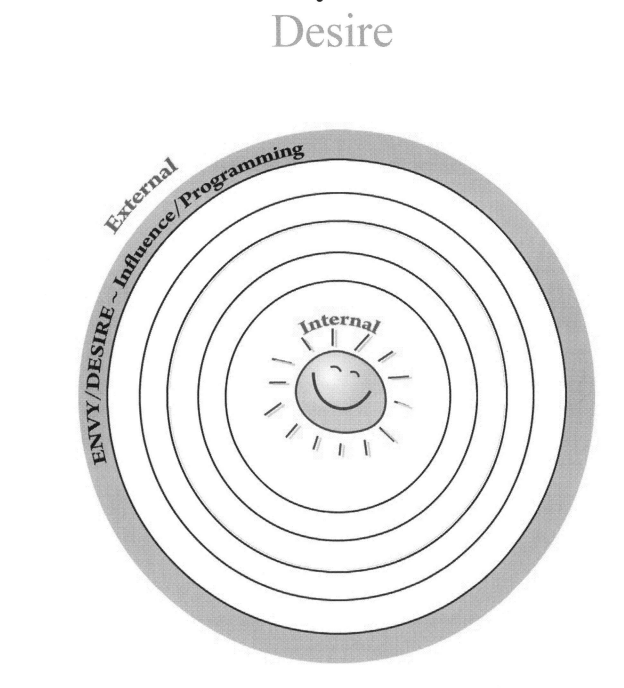

<u>Layer 1: DESIRE</u>

The DESIRE worksheet is created to help you reflect on what you believe will create more happiness in your life and WHY you believe it. It is important to know that just merely reflecting on your desires and observing whether they are authentically yours or influenced by others can help you release desires that hold you back.

1. What are the circumstances and/or things (desires) that you believe will make you happy? _____

_____

_____

_____

_____

_____

2. Why do you believe that those circumstances will create happiness?

_____

_____

_____

3. Are any of the above influenced primarily by your society, friends, or upbringing? If yes, which ones? _____

_____

_____

_____

4. Are your AUTHENTIC desires different than the above? If so, what are they?

_____

_____

_____

_____

Reflection: Don't give away your power

If a change you are trying to make isn't working, like creating more joy and happiness, it may be that you are trying to change the wrong thing. You are probably doing things and creating desires because you think you "should" and not because you really want to. You're probably doing it because someone else thinks it's what is best, or in order to please someone, or to avoid being rejected. Making decisions based on what others think is giving away your power.

Do you find yourself resisting change for any of the following reasons?

__Fear of repercussions from others

__Guilt over hurting someone else

__Guilt over disappointing another

__Fear of being judged, criticized, or rejected

List things that you do that you don't want to do or things you want to do but don't:	Describe in what way, if any, you are choosing to do these things because of someone else:

To evaluate how much of your power you give away, consider the reasons that you do what you do, or rather don't do what you want.

Do you find a strong correlation between the areas of your life you are unsatisfied with and the areas of your life you allow others to determine for you? In the Your Life Movie activity (See Layer 6: Emotions), did you determine that you allow others to write your screen play? If so, we urge you to strongly consider whether you are willing to continue to allow other people to limit your life.

Check off any area in which you **<u>ARE</u>** WILLING to allow others to control your life:

__What I do for a living

__Who I date or marry

__Where I live

__What I wear or look like

__How I spend my time

__How I raise my children

__What I believe

__What I say

__Whether or not I have what I want in life

__Whether or not I reach my potential

Be honest with yourself. If you are not willing, but you find you are doing it anyway, are you willing to make THIS change – and to take back your power?   __Yes! __No

Layer 2
Limiting Beliefs

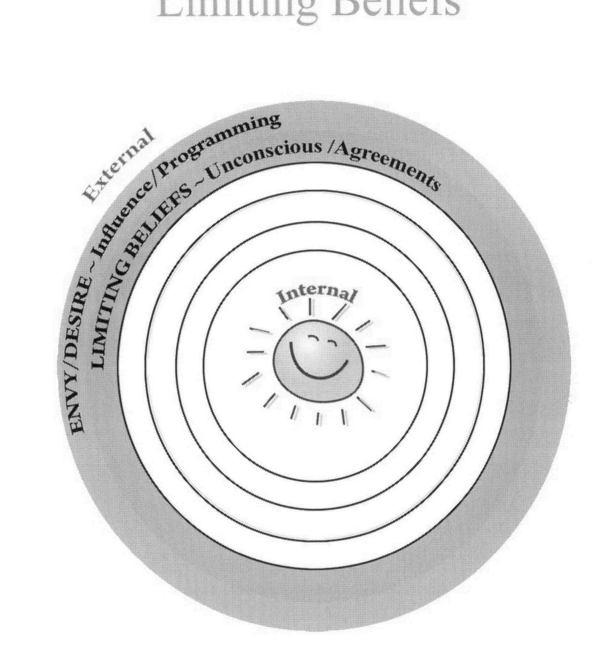

Layer 2: Limiting Beliefs

We are often unaware of our limiting beliefs because they were "passed down" to us by the attitudes and beliefs of others. As long as they remain unconscious (we are not aware of them) they can hold us back from achieving our fullest potential and experiencing joy. For example, if we have heard all of our life that money is the root of evil then we may unconsciously create situations that limit our financial success out of fear of that evil.

Below is a list of some common "phrases" that we are often told growing up or hear in our community. They are so "normal" that we rarely question their validity or consider how they affect our belief systems or make us unhappy. Of course, there is some truth and a good intention behind most of them, but consider which ones you have been conditioned to believe and how they have impacted your beliefs and your life.

"Money is the root of all evil."
Good intention: money does not bring happiness and can corrupt
Conditioned fear: negative association with having money; it turns you into a bad person
Potential limits: unconsciously avoiding or sabotaging financial success to avoid the "negative qualities" you believe you'll develop if you have money

"Finish your plate. There are starving people in the world."
Good intention: don't be wasteful with food and have compassion for others
Conditioned fear: food scarcity or guilt for having more opportunity than others
Potential limits: over eating and health problems or holding yourself back to avoid feeling guilty over having more opportunity than others

"Money doesn't grow on trees."
Good intention: be intelligent with how you spend your money
Conditioned fear: money scarcity; feeling that there is not enough and it is hard to get
Potential limits: not believing you can have what you want if it involves having money and therefore not going for it

"Don't burn your bridges."

Good intention: keep good relationships with people who may one day be a resource

Conditioned fear: apprehension to do what you know is right for you if you feel it will make someone disapprove of or reject you

Potential limits: not making a change or taking an opportunity when it comes out of fear of disappointing, offending, or otherwise burning a bridge

"No pain no gain."

Good intention: the reward is worth the struggle

Conditioned fear: the belief that in order to be successful one must suffer

Potential limits: choosing not to make changes or go for what you want because you feel it will be difficult or painful, holding yourself back from success

"Life is hard."

Good intention: pain and struggle are a normal part of being human

Conditioned fear: there is no hope of you feeling at ease or happy in life

Potential limits: feeling discouraged and hopeless; accepting difficulties or unnecessary suffering because you believe it is normal or expected

"Honor thy mother and father."

Good intention: treat your parents with respect and be grateful for them

Conditioned fear: overly concerned about disappointing your parents or that you will be disowned if you follow your heart

Potential limits: holding yourself back from what you want and know you need to do or who you are because your parents (or others) do not approve

"No one ever said life is fair."

Good intention: sometimes things seem unfair, but it is okay

Conditioned fear: you will not get what you deserve and there is no justice in the world

Potential limits: you may hold yourself back feeling like it will not pay off or you may develop feelings of hopelessness

"Good things come to those who wait."

Good intention: it is important to be patient and it's worth the wait

Conditioned fear: you have to wait a long time to get what you want

Potential limits: a feeling of impatience due to focusing on the length of time and not doing something you want because it will "take too long"

"You have to pay your dues."

Good intention: it takes effort to get results

Conditioned fear: you will have to suffer in order to be worthy of any pay off

Potential limits: feeling unworthy, you may not take opportunities or you may punish yourself for rewards and accomplishments you receive with ease

"Speak only when spoken to."

Good intention: be polite and don't interrupt

Conditioned fear: apprehension to approach others or speak up

Potential limits: avoidance of activities or circumstances requiring you to be in authority, lead, demand what you want, stand up for what you believe, or speak in front of others

"Children are meant to be seen and not heard."

Good intention: really, there is no good intention here

Conditioned fear: feelings of being unworthy and low self-esteem

Potential limits: avoidance of being in the spotlight or anything that would make you feel important or valued

Which of these phrases were you conditioned to believe?

_____

_____

_____

Can you think of others?

_____

_____

_____

Do you believe they are all true?   __Yes   __No

Can you see any fears you developed because of them?

_____

_____

_____

Can you see any way in which they have limited you?

_____

_____

_____

Can you see how you would be happier with different beliefs? How?

_____

_____

_____

What are some new beliefs you'd prefer to have instead?

_____

_____

_____

_____

_____

_____

_____

_____

_____

_____

_____

Changing Your Perspective by Changing Your WORDS!

Perspective is everything when it comes to how we feel, and the words that we use are critical factors of our perspective. Below are some examples of key words that, if changed, will drastically impact our unconscious minds. The shift may seem small, but it can have a drastic effect on our happiness and our overall motivation.

Have To vs. Get To:

What areas in your life do you feel and say "I have to"? For example: "I have to go to work." Change it to "I get to go to work," and see how different you feel. Now, change YOUR "have to's" into "get to's" and try your new perspective on for size.

I have to:_____

I get to:_____

I have to:_____

I get to:_____

I have to:_____

I get to:_____

I Can't vs. How Can I?

What areas do you limit your ability to truly be authentic to what you want and your ability to feel joy? Changing this terminology allows the brain to stop shutting off possibilities and instead look for ways to create the things you desire. What do you feel limited about? Does asking "How can I?" change the way you feel about it?

I can't:_____

How can I:_____

I can't:_____

How can I:_____

I can't:_____

How can I:_____

Changing Your "What if's"!

Many times we use "What if's" in a negative way. For example, people say "What if I get fired", "What if my relationship goes bad", and so on and so on. These "what if's" take away our ability to feel joy because they stop us from doing what we really want in life out of fear of "what if". Try turning your "What if's" into POSITIVE ones! "What if you get a promotion?" and "What if your relationship improves?" Remember, the unconscious mind is powerful and will LOOK FOR whatever you tell it to look for. By saying "What if something amazing happened?" your mind automatically will begin scanning your life for amazing things!

What negative "what if's" do you often think? Rewrite new, positive ones below:

What If...

_____

_____

_____

What If...

_____

_____

_____

What If...

_____

_____

_____

Layer 3
Ego/Identity

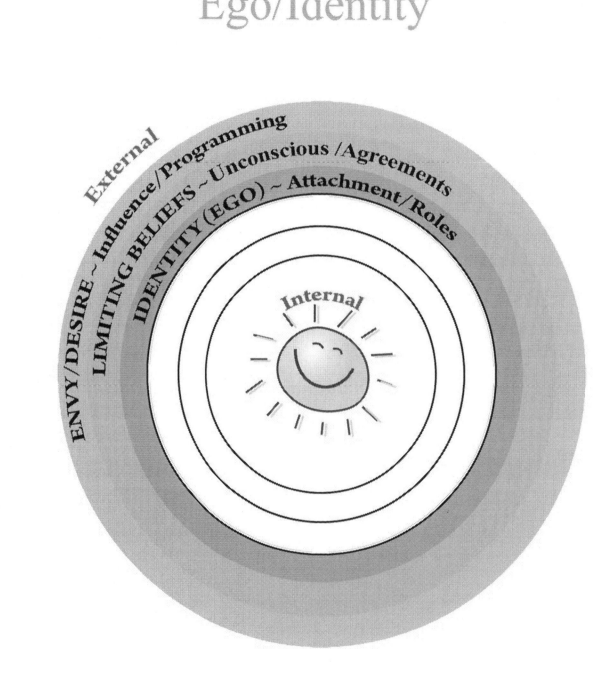

Layer 3: EGO/IDENTITY

What Roles Do You Play?

What roles did you see growing up, from your caretakers and those around you, and in what ways do you play them out the same way in your life?

_____

_____

_____

_____

_____

_____

What roles do not serve you that you would like to release?

_____

_____

_____

_____

_____

_____

What roles DO serve you that you would like to continue in your life?

_____

_____

_____

_____

_____

_____

Reflection: Who am I?

A common reason that many people resist or avoid change, even if it will improve their life, is because the issue they are trying to address has become interwoven with their self-identity. This is the case especially if the issue at hand is painful. People become attached to their pain. It becomes part of their story—what has gone wrong, what has been done to them, how they've been hurt—so much so that they think it is who they are. Notice how part of you resists letting go of the things that make you unhappy and the compulsion you have to think and talk about it. Isn't it funny how part of you gets a peculiar pleasure out of your pain?

If you hate your job, but you believe you are someone who never likes what they do for a living, you may find it difficult to find a new, more enjoyable job. You would have to give up your belief that you are someone who doesn't like work. If you are mistreated or abused by your significant other, but you believe you are someone who is always a victim, you may find it difficult to remove yourself from the relationship. You would have to give up your belief that you are a victim.

In what ways do you consider a "problem" to be part of your identity? _____

_____

_____

_____

_____

Do you talk about it a lot?

Do you get attention because of it?

Does it give you a sense of purpose?

You are NOT:

| What you do | What you have | What others think of you |
| Your past | Your problems | |

If you find that your problems, pain, or the things you are discontent with are part of your identity, ask yourself, "is this who I want to be?"

The 3 Detrimental Identities: illness, victim, poverty

Which, if any, of these are a part of your identity?

_____

_____

_____

_____

_____

What positive identity can you replace it with?

_____

_____

_____

_____

_____

The 5 Success Identities: grateful, engaged, forgiving, contributing, purposeful

How can you increase your identification with these qualities (statements and actions you can make)?

_____

_____

_____

_____

_____

Layer 4
Time (Past/Future)

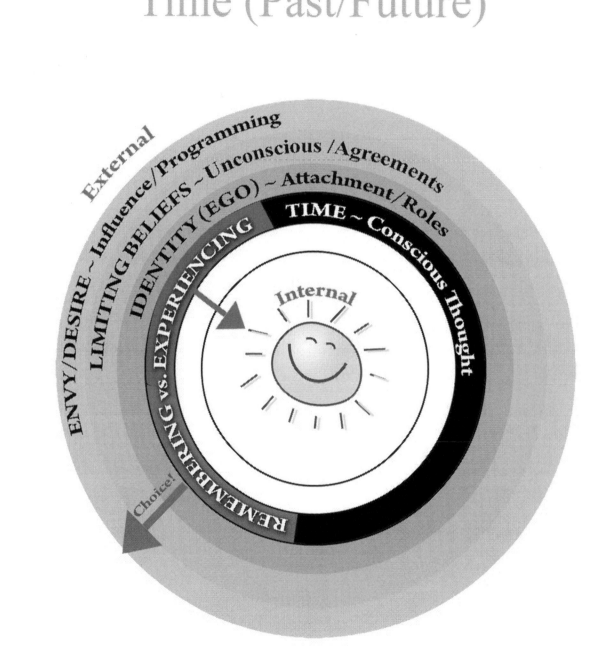

Layer 4: TIME

Vacation Activity:

I'm giving you the newest, greatest camera and have offered to make a video memoir of your trip... where would you choose to go?

_____

_____

_____

_____

_____

Now, you are able to go on any vacation you want, but you are not allowed to bring a phone or camera on your trip and your memory will be erased when you return... where would you choose to go?

_____

_____

_____

_____

_____

Many times we choose what we do with our time and energy based on people's opinion of it. Even more so humans tend to make decisions about their lives (and vacations) based on the future memories they want to have, rather than because they would truly enjoy the experience. Neither living for the moment or for the memory is bad; what matters is that you do what YOU truly want. Did your vacation destination change? Did your motives change? And if yes, why?

_____

_____

_____

_____

Layer 5
Patterns/Conditioning

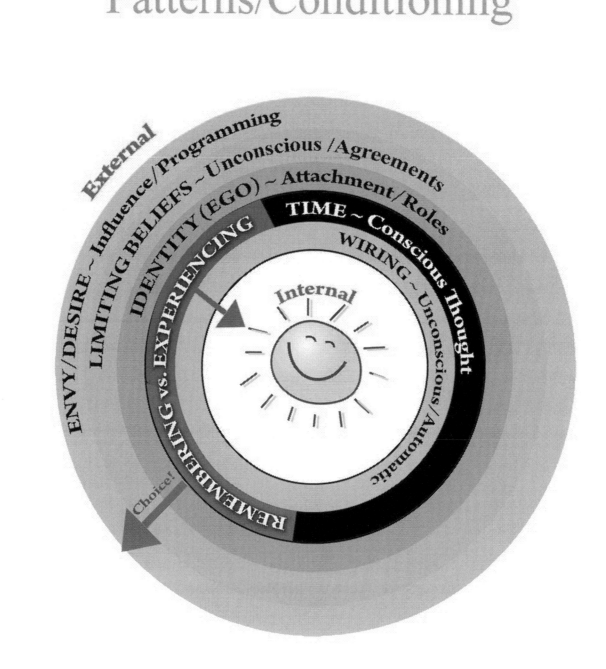

Layer 5: PATTERNS/CONDITIONING

Reflect on your life: what are some things that keep repeating themselves (patterns):

_____

_____

_____

_____

Why do they keep repeating themselves, and how could you change it?

_____

_____

_____

_____

What are some of the "triggers" that create a negative emotional response in you (words, phrases, body language, foods, actions, people, environments)?

_____

_____

_____

_____

What are some of the triggers that create a positive emotional response in you (words, phrases, body language, foods, actions, people, environments)?

_____

_____

_____

_____

Make a list of 5 things you can **do or think** in *any* moment to give yourself a Joy Boost!

1. _____
   _____

2. _____
   _____

3. _____
   _____

4. _____
   _____

5. _____
   _____

Also take a look at the things below to define what places or things can serve as a trigger for positive emotions.

Songs:

_____

_____

Places:

_____

_____

People:

_____

_____

Memories:

_____

_____

Movies/videos:

_____

_____

Now, use these positive triggers to shift your emotions to JOY whenever you want!

Get Wired for Joy:
Change Your State

The following activity and tool is from the book *Wired For Joy! A Revolutionary Method for Creating Happiness from Within* by Laurel Mellin.

When you find yourself in a state other than joy, use the following activities to switch your "stress circuit" to a "joy circuit" and feel better now!

Step 1) Recognize and accept your current state. By accepting how you feel you will not add resistance to the feeling, which only makes it worse.

Step 2) Determine what "brain state" you are currently at:

#	Brain State	Use This Tool	Effect
1	Feeling Great	Sanctuary Tool	Celebrate 1
2	Feeling Good	Feelings Check Tool	Get to 1
3	A Little Stressed	Emotional Housecleaning Tool	Get to 1
4	Definitely Stressed	Cycle Tool	Get to 1
5	Stressed Out!	Damage Control Tool	Get to 1 or 4

Step 3) Use the following tools to shift your brain state, trigger a joy wire, and re-wire for JOY!

5) Damage Control Tool (2-5 minutes)
GOAL: Calm the circuit
1) Tell yourself (or say out loud) "Do Not Judge" (self or others)
Tell yourself (or say out loud) "Minimize Harm"
Tell yourself (or say out loud) "This will pass" (It's just a wire!)
2) Repeat each phrase 10 to 20 times until you "pop" the circuit, meaning you "snap yourself out of it". You will either feel joy (level 1) or simply less stressed, in which case you can identify your state and use another tool to shift yourself higher.

4) Cycle Tool (2-5 minutes quick, 5-20 minutes deep)
GOAL: Dismantle the circuit
1) State the facts arouse the stress circuit
2) Zero in on the stress circuit (feel it)
I feel angry that...   I feel sad that...
I feel afraid that...   I feel guilty that...
What is my unreasonable expectation/belief that causes this to trigger me?
3) Build a Joy Circuit
What new, reasonable, powerful belief am I choosing for myself?
What will be the hard part of changing my belief?
What reward will I earn?
4) Reinforce the new Joy wire (grind it in) by repeating your new belief 10 times
5) Feel surge of joy

3) Emotional Housecleaning Tool (1 minute)
GOAL: Release stress
1) Express Negative Emotions (release): Cycle through all 4: I feel angry that... sad that, afraid that, guilty about...
2) Express Positive Emotions: Grateful, happy, secure, proud...
4) Feel surge of joy
*If negative feeling is too powerful or you cannot reach positive, you are in brain state 4.

2) Feelings Check Tool (1 minute)
GOAL: Don't accept mediocre!
1) Ask "How do I feel?" (label the positive or negative experience) and identify "What's my strongest feeling?"
2) Ask "What do I need?" It can be anything from "I need to eat" to "I feel lonely" or maybe "I need to relax."
3) Ask "Do I need support?" If you feel that support from another person, such as a hug or a phone call, would help, reach out and take the opportunity for intimacy.
4) Do another check-in to see if your state has shifted to Level 1 and feel a surge of joy

1) Sanctuary Tool (30 seconds)
GOAL: Appreciating your joy!
1) Lovingly observe and connect to yourself
2) Feel compassion for yourself and others
3) Feel surge of joy

For further explanation and inspiration, read *Wired For Joy!: A Revolutionary Method for Creating Happiness from Within* by Laurel Mellin.

Layer 6
Mood/Emotions

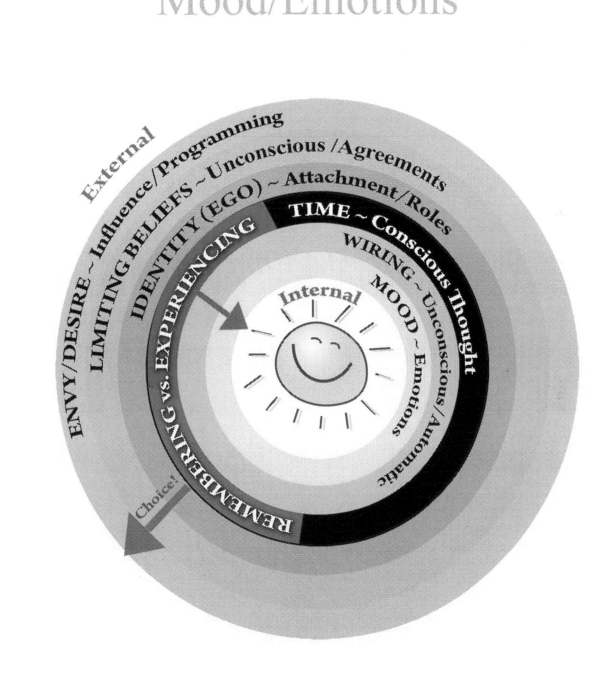

External

ENVY/DESIRE ~ Influence/Programming

LIMITING BELIEFS ~ Unconscious /Agreements

IDENTITY (EGO) ~ Attachment/Roles

REMEMBERING vs. EXPERIENCING

TIME ~ Conscious Thought

WIRING ~ Unconscious/Automatic

MOOD ~ Emotions

Internal

Choice!

Layer 6: MOOD/EMOTIONS

One of the best ways to shift our emotions to JOY is to be in a place of gratitude. Do the activity below to help you get to that place: Write at least a 300 word letter expressing gratitude to someone in your life (living) who you have unexpressed gratitude for.

Now, consider giving this to him or her and sharing your joy. ☺

Appreciation/Gratitude Journaling

One of the BEST ways to shift yourself to a positive emotional state is to start thinking of everything you APPRECIATE about life—your current situation, your self, the world, or whatever it is that is currently triggering you to not be in a positive emotional state. A great tool to use is an Appreciation or Gratitude Journal, as write down your gratitude amplifies its power. You can feel appreciation any time without journaling, however the journal can be a great way of shifting emotion or being PRE-EMPTIVE, meaning when you wake up or before bed you can writing your appreciations in your journal, which will get you into a great brain state and give you a powerful, sustainable boost of joy!

What do YOU appreciate?

ANCHORING

An anchor is a stimulus that triggers a response in you or another person. When a person reaches the peak of this intense emotional state, if a specific stimulus is applied, a link is neurologically created between the stimulus and the state. An anchored state is always a rich, fully associated psychological state or experience.

You may stimulate altered psychological states in other people without meaning to; for example, your intention may be for the best, yet may have an undesired effect. Hugging a crying person may seem like a comforting thing to do, but you are creating an 'anchored response' in that person, 'you hugging' them becomes linked to their upset state. Next time you give them a welcoming hug they may feel upset – a response that was never your intention and may be confusing to the both of you.

They occur quite naturally and unconsciously. For instance, if you have a particular song you hear that brings you back to a memory and a corresponding emotional state, that song is an anchor for you. Anchors can be visual (sight), auditory (sound), kinaesthetic (touch), olfactory/gustatory (smell/taste) or a combination of those mentioned.

When anchoring with clients, we are using TOUCH. It is important to anchor on appropriate and neutral locations, such as the knuckles or shoulders. See Keys to Successful Anchoring for additional tips.

THE FOUR STEPS TO ANCHORING

First, get into rapport with the other person. Get the person's permission to touch them.
1. Recall: Have the person recall a past, vivid, intense, desired emotional state.
2. Unique Anchor: Provide a specific stimulus as the state reaches its peak intensity. Take off the anchor before it goes over the peak.
3. State Break: Break the state with the person so their state changes (such as by asking an unrelated question)
4. Test: Test the anchor by inviting them to fire the same stimulus (touching the same point in *exactly* the same way) and watching to see that they go into the anchored state.

THE FIVE KEYS TO SUCCESSFUL ANCHORING

1. Emotional states being anchored need to be intense, vivid and powerfully felt (i.e., loved, powerful, energized, confident, falling down laughing).
2. The anchor must be applied at the exact time that the client's emotional state is increasing towards its peak. As the state reaches its peak, the anchor should be removed. It's important to remove the anchor before the peak state begins to diminish. (To leave the kinesthetic touch on beyond the peak means you will anchor a diminishing state. Removing the 'trigger' touch *before* the peak means that you anchor a 'growing' state.)
3. The stimulus used for the anchor (i.e. the touch point) must be unique, meaning it cannot be a point that is routinely touched under normal circumstances.

4. Replication: The anchor must be repeatable (in the exact same way), ideally by the client, in order to reinforce it.
5. Number of times: The more times the anchor is created the better the anchor will trigger the desired state.

PREFERRED STATES FOR ANCHORING

1. Emotional states being anchored need to be intense, vivid and powerfully felt (i.e., loved, powerful, energized, confident, falling down laughing).
2. The most intense states are those that occur naturally, e.g. laughter.
3. A single, fully associated, vivid and specific memory that they can relive again, as if now, is best.
4. Generalized memories of the past are much less intense and tend to be far less useful for anchoring purposes.
5. By far the least preferred states are imagined or constructed states, as they lack the intensity of real experiences.

STACKING ANCHORS

Sometimes a single anchor is not strong enough to get the desired psychological state in the other person. This is when we can 'stack' a number of experience 'anchors' on the same anchor point, (the kinesthetic trigger point that we touch), thereby making it sufficiently powerful. Repeat the anchor script multiple times, using a different state each time.
Ask about:
- A specific time when you felt 'Really Powerful.'
- A specific time when you felt 'Utterly Energized.'
- A specific time when you felt 'Totally Confident.'
- A specific time when you had the feeling that you could 'fall down laughing.'

EMPOWERMENT CIRCLE

This method of anchoring is a great tool for group work or virtual meetings. It also more fully engages the individual because they are moving their entire body.
1. First get into rapport with your client. Determine the desired state. Get into the desired state yourself. Access your own memories.
2. Create the circle: *"Imagine there is a circle on the floor in front of you.* [This can be referred to as a 'circle of calm' or a 'circle of power,' etc., depending on the desired state.] *In a moment I'm going to have you elicit the desired state. When you can feel the state peaking, you're going to step into the circle AND trigger an anchor somewhere on your body that you could easily do in public without being noticed, such as snapping your fingers or squeezing your thumb nail. When the intensity begins to decrease, step back out of the circle and release the anchor."*
3. Have the person recall a past, vivid, intense, desired emotional state.
"Can you remember a time when you felt totally (choose state)? "A specific time?"
"As you go back to that time now… go right back to that time, float into your body and

relive it again now. See what you saw, hear what you heard, notice what you noticed and really feel the feelings now of being totally (choose state)."

4. Anchor the Circle: Instruct the client to notice when their emotional state peaks and step into the circle while engaging their chosen anchor point and to exit the circle and release the anchor when it begins to wane.

5. State Break: Break the state with the person so their state changes (such as by asking an unrelated question). *Then, repeat the anchor.*

6. Test: Test the anchor by inviting them to fire the same stimulus (touching the same point in *exactly* the same way) and watching to see that they go into the anchored state.

Steps to Forgiveness

1. Write it down: Make a list of people you need to forgive and what you want to forgive them for. Include what you need to forgive *yourself* for. (See the other forgiveness worksheet for a complete activity for this step.)

_____

_____

_____

_____

_____

_____

2. Reflect: Acknowledge the pain that the lack of forgiveness (on your part) has caused you and how it currently impacts your life. Is it more painful than the actual experience?

_____

_____

_____

_____

_____

_____

3. Apologize: Express your apology through a letter, email, phone call, or in person. (Remember not to be attached to the results since this is about you, not them. Do not expect to be forgiven.) What will you say?

_____

_____

_____

_____

_____

_____

4. Express grievances: If there are items on your forgiveness list that you have never addressed with the person, approach them about it. There may be a misunderstanding behind the situation, or you may receive an apology. (Do not be attached to the outcome. Express yourself for its own sake.)

_____

_____

_____

_____

_____

_____

5. Learn the lessons: What are some things that you can learn from the situations? Are there any positives that have or can come out of the experiences? What lessons could the other person(s) have learned?

_____
_____
_____
_____
_____
_____

6. Let go: Release any expectations from anyone else. This includes expectations of forgiveness or apologies from others or changes in others' behaviors. Forgiving doesn't mean accepting unacceptable behavior, but if the person does not change it is your responsibility to do what's right for you, even if it means cutting ties with the person. What expectations do you release?

_____
_____
_____
_____
_____
_____

7. Reprogram your mind: Create an action plan on how to shift your resentful thoughts when negative feelings come up. Even once you forgive old mental patterns may be retriggered. Write down what you will tell yourself to remind yourself of your forgiveness and refocus back to your true desires.

_____
_____
_____
_____
_____
_____

8. Live and be free! Forgiveness is about personal power. A life well lived is your best revenge; therefore take your power back and focus on your desires. Don't do it because, "You'll show them," do it because you want to live your life with freedom and passion. Forgiveness is often an opportunity to learn, grow, and heal. We may even find that the negative experiences were blessings in disguise if we can create a place for forgiveness and acceptance in our hearts. Remember forgiveness is 100 percent your responsibility. Only you can unlock the door to your prison and shift your life from limitation to freedom.

Made in the USA
Lexington, KY
13 July 2019